Laurie Krasny Brown

Baby Time

A Grownup's Handbook to Use with Baby

pictures by Marc Brown

Alfred A. Knopf · New York

To Eliza, Our Inspiration

THIS IS A BORZOI BOOK PUBLISHED BY ALFRED A. KNOPF, INC.

Copyright © 1989 by Laurene Krasny Brown and Marc Brown.
All rights reserved under International and Pan-American Copyright Conventions.
Published in the United States by Alfred A. Knopf, Inc., New York,
and simultaneously in Canada by Random House of Canada Limited, Toronto.
Distributed by Random House, Inc., New York.

Manufactured in the United States of America
2 4 6 8 9 7 5 3 1

Library of Congress Cataloging-in-Publication Data
Brown, Laurene Krasny.
Baby time / by Laurene Krasny Brown ; illustrated by Marc Brown.
p. cm.
ISBN 0-394-89462-6   ISBN 0-394-99462-0 (lib. bdg.)
1. Infants. 2. Child rearing. I. Title.   HQ774.B78   1989
649′.122—dc19   88-34901

Special thanks for their generous advice to Dr. Larry Cohan,
pediatrician and teacher of pediatrics,
and Dr. Howard Gardner, professor of education
and adjunct professor of neurology.

INTRODUCTION

BABY TIME was inspired by the birth of our daughter. Years of academic training and professional experience in child development did surprisingly little to prepare me for the intense feelings that came with her birth. It seems a privilege—if also the weightiest responsibility—to witness daily the gradual unfolding of a new life and have the chance to contribute to that baby's development.

But it's a very personal matter, making the most of the time you and your baby have together. From one day to the next you learn to recognize the kinds of attention your baby needs, and you discover ways to encourage his health, growth, and good spirits. The more confident you become as a parent, the better nurturing you can provide. *Baby Time* is a resource to help you build that confidence.

It helps to have good information about how infants develop. The insights offered here can better enable you to understand how a given form of behavior reflects your baby's progress. Patience comes much more easily when you can celebrate each tiny achievement as a step along the way to greater maturity.

The best way to develop your intuitive sense is by spending time with your baby, paying good attention to what he does, and taking cues from him. *Baby Time* suggests all kinds of things to do with a baby. Each of the five senses is discussed separately to illustrate how closely your baby's experience is tied to the way things look, sound, smell, taste, feel, and move. Of course, in reality all the senses work together; in fact, one of baby's developmental tasks is to coordinate the use of the senses.

The activities pictured here were carefully selected to show you how the simplest things you do with your baby can have value and contribute to his growing awareness. Just as important, they present opportunities for having fun together. There is value in that alone.

Best of all, this is a book to enjoy reading *with* your baby. Most infants are ready to look at pictures as soon as they can hold up their heads well, and they especially like seeing pictures of other babies.

So get comfortable with baby. Some dialogue is suggested, but other comments will no doubt come to mind as you look through the book—*you* will know best what to say. Skip around and return to pages you both like. When you have finished reading, pick and choose from these ideas and add your own.

Most of all, relax and enjoy time with your baby!

Laurie Krasny Brown

SEE

No sight interests a new baby more than a human face. Let your baby study your face often. Make eye contact, and soon he will reward you with his first smile.

It takes babies longer, however, to learn that people continue to exist even when we can't see them. Peekaboo lets a baby of six months or older experiment with this notion while playing a game with you.

Where's the mommy?
Peekaboo!
There's the mommy!

FACES

If you change your appearance, a younger baby, who is still learning to recognize your face, may become confused. Reassure him by trying on and taking off glasses, hats, and the like for him.

Keep in mind that until babies are a few months old they are nearsighted and can focus only on objects about eight to twelve inches away. Not incidentally, this is the distance between baby's eyes and the face of whoever feeds him.

Mommy.

Mommy wears a hat.

Still mommy!

Baby in the mirror.

Lady with glasses.

Man on TV.

Puppet.

THINGS TO SEE

A baby learns most from things that interest her. Notice what attracts her attention; then tell her its name, talk about it, and, if possible, let her get close to it or handle it.

You can surprise your baby by varying the things you put into a bag or box for her to discover.

What's in the box?

A tube to look through.

Shadow.

Cat at the window.

PICTURES

Once your baby holds her head up, you can begin showing her pictures. As she gets older, pictures will help her to identify all kinds of things within and beyond her world.

You can use pictures to name an item, say what it does, and describe its parts, sounds, size, color, and anything else that might interest baby.

Red, red tomatoes.

Truck to drive.

See the baby?

What does the cow say?

Baby and his family.

Another baby!

Supper for the dog.

Baby crawling.

Bunnies on baby's dish.

THINGS THAT MOVE

A young baby is more likely to notice an object if it moves. If it has bright colors and makes a noise, all the better. You can interest a baby in many things by moving them and making up sounds for them.

Roly-poly ball.

CHORES

Bring baby with you when you do household chores. Tell her what you're doing, and, as she gets older, let her help. You may appreciate simple tasks in new ways when you see them through baby's curious eyes.

If baby is not to help, have toys or books on hand. A special drawer just for baby that is filled with toys and safe household gadgets will keep an older baby happily occupied.

This is the way we fold our clothes, fold our clothes...

A cracker just for baby.

What's in the drawer for baby?

Baby jumps.   Mommy cooks.

OUT AND ABOUT

Dress baby for the weather. Even a stroll around the block can present endless opportunities to show him the world.

Be excited about as many new things as you can; your reaction to something unfamiliar influences how your baby feels about it.

One day baby will begin pointing out things to you. Then you will see how powerful a little index finger can be.

Ooh, ladybug! It must be spring.

In autumn the leaves blow in the wind.

Baby swings in the summer. Wheee!

The snow is cold. Brrr!

SHOPPING

Trips to stores can be a treat for all the senses. Take advantage of your shopping trips with baby by pointing out to him bits of the scenery. Try to find him a little souvenir to enjoy along the way.

See the fish swimming.

Shiny red apples taste good.

Hear the money machine.

Baby has a flower to sniff.

HEAR

No sound interests a new baby more than a human voice. Your young baby will soon follow the sound of your voice with her eyes and listen intently while you speak.

The more you talk with your baby, the more talkative baby is likely to be. She will practice babbling even when alone and enjoy hearing her own voice.

Baby is happy to hear her daddy's voice.

SOUNDS TO HEAR

Help your baby learn about a sound by calling her attention to it, imitating it, and naming its source.

The toilet flushes. Whoosh! Glub glub goes the water.

Brring brring! The telephone rings.

Whirrr! The blender spins.

The dog barks. Woof! Woof! Woof!

SOUNDS TO MAKE

Once a baby can hold on to things with his hands, he will love making noise with them. Encourage him to produce all kinds of sounds.

Invent rattles by filling safe containers with dried beans, buttons, bells, and coins.

Everyday things you may take for granted will delight your baby as toys.

Babies shake their rattles. Shake shake shake!

Baby bang bang banging on his tray.

Shhh. Now baby taps softly. Tap. Tap. Tap.

Pat-a-cake, pat-a-cake, baker's man.

CONVERSATION

Good conversation requires listening as well as speaking. Comment on things baby sees or does, and give him time to respond in his own way. Try repeating the sounds he makes. Then baby will know you've been listening.

Refer to your baby by name. It will help both of you learn that he's a person in his own right.

Tape-record baby's voice from time to time and play it back. You'll appreciate his progress. Be sure to save the recording for him!

TONE OF VOICE

To an infant how you speak is more important than what you say. Your tone of voice shows your feelings and can influence baby's behavior. An angry, shouting voice often upsets a calm baby, whereas a soft, gentle voice can calm down an upset baby.

GESTURES SPEAK TOO

Babies can express themselves long before they learn to talk. They communicate with you using facial expressions, gestures, and sounds. Sometimes you have to "listen" with your eyes!

READING AND RHYMING

Get in the habit of reading books and magazines to baby every day. This will foster a love for books and an eagerness to learn to read later on. Remember, "reading" to baby can mean just pointing out the pictures on the page.

Fit rhymes into everyday routines whenever you can. Listening to rhymes helps develop baby's language skills. Keep handy a copy of Mother Goose and other rhyme books. Have fun thinking up nonsense words to rhyme and repeat.

Daddy reads to baby and his brother.

MUSIC AND DANCE

Babies are never too young to be introduced to music and dance. They like tunes with a simple beat and clear melody. Try singing along, clapping, or moving baby's body to the beat. Play recordings of nursery rhymes and children's songs. Bring tapes along on car trips. Let baby sample live music at a parade or outdoor concert.

Sing to your baby. The simplest, silliest tunes will please her, especially if you sing them. Treat her to a lullaby at bedtime.

Mommies and daddies make music too.

Skip, skip, skip to my Lou...

Row, row, row your boat gently down the stream...

Rock-a-bye, baby, on the treetop...

TASTE AND SMELL

Feeding is baby's first and most important experience of taste and smell, two closely related senses. A baby's feeding also satisfies much more than hunger: by being fed on time and given enough time to suck, by being held, smiled at, and enjoyed, a baby learns to trust the people in his world.

Baby sucks his milk.

THINGS TO SMELL

Help your baby to enjoy fragrant things by
showing her how to sniff. She may want to
taste good-smelling things whether or not
they are edible, so be prepared to act quickly!

Daddy and baby sniff a flower. Mmm!

Warm muffins smell good.

Ugh! Baby doesn't like that smell.

Baby sniffs puppy. And puppy sniffs baby.

EATING

Offer your older baby balanced meals and let him taste and smell many different foods. Introduce new dishes one at a time. Be excited about meals and show baby that you will try what you feed him. Don't force him to eat a food; instead, try it another time and perhaps in another form.

Baby can feed himself finger food while you help with a spoon. Later he can practice getting a small spoon to his mouth by himself.

CHEESE

MEATBALLS

SCRAMBLED EGG

FISH CAKE

COOKIE

BROCCOLI FLOWER

PEAS

GREEN BEAN

PEANUT BUTTER ON BREAD

BONED CHICKEN

MUFFIN

CARROTS

RICE

CEREAL

CRACKER

NOODLE

GRAPES

POTATO WEDGE

PEAR

Try some carrots, baby.

BANANA

BERRIES

APPLE

THINGS TO MOUTH

Being the oral creature she is, your baby gets to know a thing by putting it in her mouth. If you use a pacifier, give baby plenty of time without it. Make safe objects available. Objects must be unbreakable, too big to swallow, nontoxic, without sharp edges, and with no parts that come off or can reach the back of her throat.

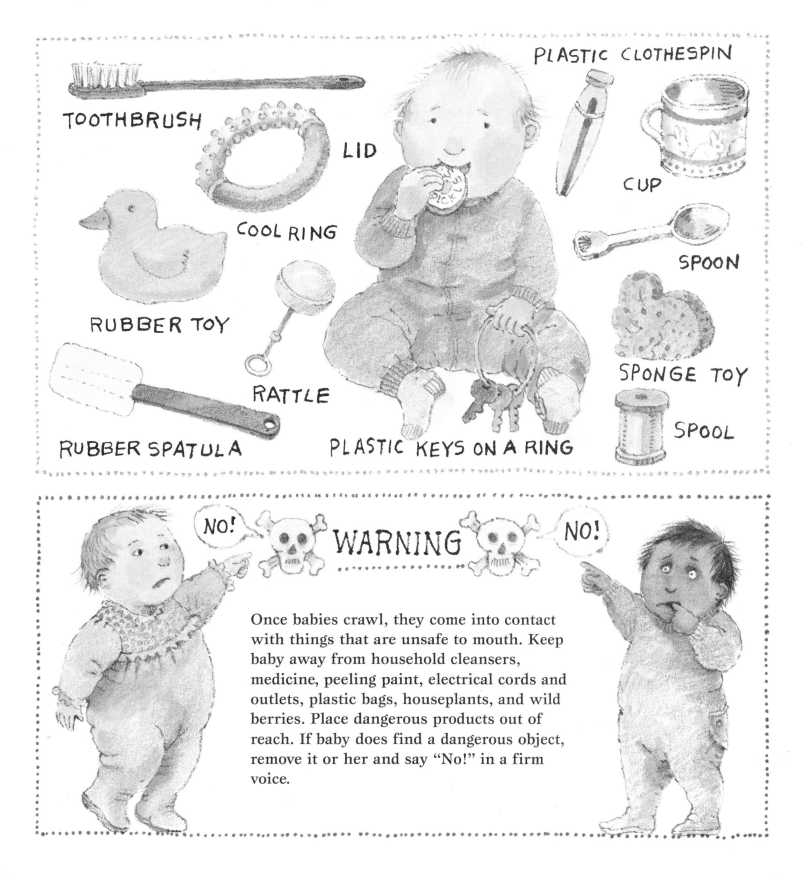

TOOTHBRUSH

COOL RING

RUBBER TOY

RUBBER SPATULA

RATTLE

LID

PLASTIC KEYS ON A RING

PLASTIC CLOTHESPIN

CUP

SPOON

SPONGE TOY

SPOOL

NO! WARNING NO!

Once babies crawl, they come into contact with things that are unsafe to mouth. Keep baby away from household cleansers, medicine, peeling paint, electrical cords and outlets, plastic bags, houseplants, and wild berries. Place dangerous products out of reach. If baby does find a dangerous object, remove it or her and say "No!" in a firm voice.

TOUCH

Being in close physical contact with you comforts your baby and helps him feel safe. The more physically secure he feels, the more eager he will be to reach out and explore his surroundings.

As baby learns to look forward to your cuddles and hugs, he will also begin returning your affection. Somehow, magically, all those sleepless nights seem a small price to pay for his love.

Baby rubs noses with sister.

SELF-DISCOVERY

Babies feel warm or cold; they may hurt; they get hungry. They experience closeness with others. In time they become aware of their physical self: two hands, two feet, two ears, a tummy, perhaps hair.... They explore and try out their bodies.

Baby plays with her hands.

Kick, baby, kick!
What a clever trick!

Baby pats his tummy.

Hmm, tasty toes.

BATH TIME

Encourage your baby to play in the tub and enjoy the sensual feel of warm water, nubby cloth, tickly bubbles, a slippery ball, and so on.

Very young infants need only their faces, hands, and bottoms washed every day. Introduce your baby gradually to bathing in a small tub and don't worry if she resists once in a while.

Rub-a-dub-dub,
It's fun in the tub!

Squish! goes the sponge.

Wrap up baby.
Pat her dry.

This little piggy went to market...

HOW TO MASSAGE A BABY

Babies enjoy and benefit from massage. It relaxes baby's muscles, exercises joints, and promotes circulation, digestion, and body awareness. Massage all parts of her body. Vary your touch from gentle strokes to firm rubbing or kneading. Try to keep movements slow and rhythmic. Relax and take your time. After baby's bath is a nice time for a massage.

1. Moisten hands with baby oil. Use up and out motions on shoulders.

2. Massage down and away from heart on lower chest.

3. Stroke and knead each arm.

4. Slowly press thumb up each hand. Rub each finger.

5. Stroke and knead each leg.

6. Don't forget feet. Rub and wiggle each toe.

7. Rub and stroke back.

8. Massage temples.

9. When you finish, remove hands slowly and give baby a hug and kiss.

TOUCHING OTHERS

Your baby will learn how to touch others by the way you handle him. Let him know if he hurts you unintentionally. Showing baby how to be considerate of living things helps him learn to be loving and humane.

Mommy's mouth. Nibble, nibble at baby's finger.

Baby wants to pet the cat.

Baby hugs teddy.

No, no, baby. Don't pull uncle's beard.

THINGS TO TOUCH

Let your baby discover different textures by touching and comparing opposite things that are smooth or rough, hard or soft, wet or dry. Make him aware of a thing's shape, temperature, and weight.

Babies love to handle paper. Let your baby tear, rustle, crumple, and study paper to his heart's content. (But be sure he doesn't swallow any!)

Soft feather.

Squishy sand.

Sticky tape.

Bumpy shoe bottoms.

MOVEMENT

Wearing your baby in a frontpack lets her enjoy your body warmth and heartbeat and the motion of your footsteps—while you have both hands free!

Your baby will take her first steps when she is ready. She will want to practice often. You can help by providing safe spaces, sturdy things to hold on to, and patience to let her explore.

WAYS TO TRAVEL

There are many ways to transport your baby from place to place. Choose the one that is most convenient and pleasant for the situation.

Basket

Backpack

Car seat

Walker

Bicycle seat

Stroller

Frontpack

Carriage

Piggyback

MOVING WITH HELP

Physical movement can soothe or stimulate your baby, so be aware of what sorts of activities you introduce. Balance boisterous play with gentle cuddling. After a long stroller ride, an older baby may welcome the chance to crawl around.

MOVING WITH RHYME

Treat your baby to action rhymes. Babies enjoy both the feel of rhythmic motions and the sound of rhyming words. It is a winning combination for infants, and one that serves both physical and language development. Repeat the rhymes your baby especially likes; there is added pleasure in going through familiar motions again and again.

ACTION CONCEPTS

Allow your baby more and more opportunities to act independently. By watching her, you can judge when to offer help and when to let her try doing things herself. Encourage her to persist at a task, if only for another minute. Praise good effort as well as success.

Light off!

Light on!

Ball up!

Baby throws ball down!

ACTION CONCEPTS

Don't be discouraged when baby starts to empty shelves and drawers. First she enjoys just taking things out; later she will learn to replace them.

Out comes a little shirt!

In goes a blue sock!

Baby opens the box!

Can baby close the box? Yes, she can!

IMITATION

Babies learn a great deal from watching and trying to copy what the people around them do. Show your baby how to comb his hair or put a toy back on the shelf. To him, practicing such simple tasks is more play than chore, and it starts him off learning responsible behavior. Be careful what you do in front of his curious eyes, though; he may also imitate behavior you didn't intend him to learn!

Mommy and Daddy wave bye-bye! So does baby!

Make a face, baby.

No cream on pajamas!

Baby brushes her hair.

PHYSICAL MILESTONES

Every baby matures at his own rate. Savor each tiny step in your baby's development. Notice how his behavior changes and celebrate progress. There's no need to rush. Motor skills develop in a logical order that includes the following stages.

WHOLE BODY SKILLS

Holds up head

Sits supported

Rolls over

Rocks on hands and feet

Sits without support

Crawls or creeps

Pulls up to stand

Cruises holding on

Stands alone

First steps

HAND SKILLS

Grasps small object with palm and fingers

Reaches with two hands

Holds and shakes object with thumb and fingers

Reaches with one hand

Holds object with thumb and forefinger

Drops object on purpose

Transfers object hand to hand

Pokes with forefinger

Manipulates object

PLAYTHINGS

A baby's attention to most objects is short-lived. Select toys that interest your baby and help develop his skills in playing with them. Look around the house for safe things for baby to handle. Household objects are often more fun for him than store-bought toys. Mix and match objects. Rotate playthings by keeping some out of sight. Sell, save, give away, or discard toys as your baby outgrows them.

soft animal

cups

rattle

squeak toy

walker wagon

soft blocks

cradle gym

doll

safety mirror

ball

paper

tube

spools

strainer

bubbles

jack·in·the·box

PLAYTHINGS

When you give a new toy to your baby, show
him how it works or what it can do.

From time to time, wash baby's playthings
in hot, sudsy water.

bag	toothbrush	boat	tambourine
keys	car	books	purse
box	spoons	puppet	tea set
mobile	action figure	pan and water	crayons

But one plaything is the favorite of all babies —
you!